EDGE
BOOKS™

# SPORTS TO THE EXTREME

# EXTREME
# Air Sports

BY ERIN K. BUTLER

CAPSTONE PRESS
a capstone imprint

Edge Books are published by Capstone Press,
1710 Roe Crest Drive, North Mankato, Minnesota 56003
www.mycapstone.com

**Library of Congress Cataloging-in-Publication Data**
Library of Congress Cataloging-in-Publication data is available on the Library of Congress website.
ISBN 978-1-5157-7861-5 (library binding)
ISBN 978-1-5157-7865-3 (eBook PDF)

**Editorial Credits**
Nikki Ramsay, editor; Sara Radka, designer; Laura Manthe, production specialist

**Photo Credits**
Getty Images: Aurora Open/Craig Moore, back cover, 19, Flickr RF/Rick Neves, 17, Laureus/David Cannon,
27, (bottom), Moment Open/Jessie Reeder, 14; iStockphoto: German-skydiver, cover, grafikeray, Vitalalp, 15;
Newscom: EPA/AZHAR RAHIM, 5, Sipa USA/Abaca Press, 29, ZUMA Press/Jay Nemeth, 11, ZUMA Press/Nikos
Pilos, 26; Shutterstock: Alexandra Lande, 22, Burben, 21, Eunika Sopotnicka, 6, (bottom), Germanskydiver, 9,
LeoBrogioni, 27, (top), Mauricio Graiki, 13, natalia_maroz, 6, (top), Sergei Bachlakov, 25, Sky Antonio, 10

Graphic elements by Book Buddy Media.

Printed in the United States of America.
010364F17

# Table of Contents

# Extreme Air Sports

The sun beats down on your face as you feel the wind whipping through your hair. The ground feels miles (kilometers) away, and your heart is pumping faster than you thought possible. You are excited, but you also know there is danger. And that danger is thrilling. This is the world of extreme air sports.

Extreme air sports are not your average athletic events. They are high-speed, high-risk sports performed in the air. The people who perform them thrive on seeking thrills and getting their adrenaline pumping by defying gravity.

The world of extreme air sports is a highly specialized one. Most extreme air sports require equipment, such as harnesses, specially designed ropes, suits, gliders, or even planes. With so many diverse and exciting air sports to choose from, there is lots of room for creativity.

## EXTREME FACT!

Extreme sports can be dangerous. Between 2000 and 2011, they led to more than 4 million injuries in the United States. Injuries ranged from strains and sprains to broken bones, concussions, and traumatic brain injuries.

BASE jumpers leap from tall structures all around the world, such as the Kuala Lumpur Tower in Malaysia.

Bungee jumpers need to make sure their ropes are the right length so they will not hit the ground.

## THE BIGGEST JUMP

The Royal Gorge Bridge in Canon City, Colorado, is the highest place to bungee jump. This suspension bridge offers a jump of 1,053 feet (321 meters). However, the park has recently stopped allowing jumpers.

# CHAPTER 1

# Bungee Jumping

Today bungee jumping has become a popular and well-known activity. Many people — not just athletes — go bungee jumping for fun. It involves jumping from a high place, with an elastic cord attached to your body or ankles. The cord stops you just before you reach the ground. Different types of jumps can be performed to vary the experience of the fall. The bravest jumpers leap at night, blind to what may be in front of — or below — them.

Bungee jumping was first practiced on Pentecost Island, in the South Pacific. People would jump from tall heights with vines wrapped around their ankles. Later, thrill-seeking adventurers replaced the vines with rubber elastic cords.

Over the years, bungee jumping has evolved into the extreme sport we know today. And extreme athletes are always looking for ways to raise the stakes. For example, they may perform jumps without an extra safety harness or jump headfirst rather than feetfirst or backwards.

## EXTREME FACT!

South African athlete Mohr Keet holds the record for being the world's oldest bungee jumper. He performed a jump at the age of 96.

# CHAPTER 2

# Skydiving

When people think of extreme sports, skydiving is often one of the first things that come to mind. Nothing sounds more outrageous than jumping out of a plane with only a parachute to guide you to safety! Some people do this as a one-time activity just for fun. Others spend years practicing their craft to become truly extreme skydivers.

Modern parachuting began in France in the late 1700s. In 1797 a man named André-Jacques Garnerin began jumping from hot-air balloons and landing with a parachute. Later, people started to use airplanes instead of hot-air balloons. As plane technology improved, the height a skydiver could jump from went up too. Today extreme skydivers jump from planes flying at **altitudes** as high as 15,000 feet (4,600 m).

Competitive skydiving dates back to the 1930s. The first World Parachuting Championships took place in 1951, in what was then Yugoslavia. Today skydivers can compete in a number of different ways. Some try to reach the highest speeds possible. Others try to land on small targets. In some competitions, skydivers make formations in a group or perform special acrobatic moves while falling.

**altitude**—how high a place is above sea level

New skydivers train by leaping out of planes with experienced jumpers.

Sometimes a group of skydivers will jump in formation. Holding each others' hands and feet, divers can make interesting shapes as they fall.

There's more to skydiving than just jumping. The standard falling position is belly-to-earth. In this position, the skydiver jumps with his or her stomach facing the ground. Once a skydiver jumps out of the plane, he or she is in freefall until the parachute is deployed. Freefall can last from 40 to 85 seconds. Extreme skydivers can reach high falling speeds. The average speed is between 110 and 130 miles (177 and 209 kilometers) per hour. World records for skydiving speeds in competitions are even higher — more than 370 miles (595 km) per hour!

A skydiver needs a lot of equipment to stay safe. The most important piece of equipment is the parachute, also called the main canopy. The parachute and the reserve parachute are held in a backpack called the container. A skydiver wears the container with shoulder and leg straps attached.

When the skydiver is ready to deploy the parachute, he or she throws a small parachute, called the pilot chute. The pilot chute unfolds. As it catches the air, it pulls the main canopy out of the container and allows the diver to float gently to the ground.

## SUPER SPEED

In 2012 Felix Baumgartner set the record for the world's highest skydive. He jumped from 128,000 feet (39,014 m), reaching speeds of nearly 730 miles (1,175 km) per hour. It took him 4 minutes, 22 seconds to reach Earth's surface.

# Freeflying

Over the years, many different types of skydiving have been invented. One of the most extreme and popular types is freeflying, which began in the 1990s. In freeflying, skydivers use traditional skydiving positions, but they also extend into a vertical position while in freefall. This means that they fall faster on average than a skydiver. And unlike skydiving, which can be done by almost anyone with assistance, freeflying takes years of training to master.

In freeflying skydivers can use different jump orientations to fall either headfirst or feetfirst. Some freeflying skydivers start out in the belly-to-earth position, known as box position. Others use different positions, such as back flying, head-up flying, head-down flying, and side flying. Then, the skydiver extends his or her legs to fall straight down in a vertical position.

A skydiver must have lots of practice to begin freeflying. When freeflying, skydivers can reach an average speed of more than 160 miles (257 km) per hour. These high speeds make this type of skydiving even more dangerous.

## EXTREME FACT!

The most advanced freeflying positions, such as head-down and sit flying, can allow a jumper to fall more than 200 miles (322 km) per hour.

To start freeflying, an athlete must first master standard skydiving.

# CHAPTER 3

# BASE Jumping

For some athletes, skydiving was not extreme enough. They decided to up the stakes by inventing BASE jumping. Instead of leaping from a plane, jumps are made from stationary objects — buildings, antenna towers, spans, also known as bridges, and earth. Like skydiving, parachutes are used. But BASE jump locations are much closer to the ground. This means there is not much time to deploy a parachute.

Buildings, antenna towers, and spans are manmade, and it can be difficult to gain access to them for jumping. The last type, earth, includes natural formations, such as cliffs and mountainsides.

In many places, BASE jumping is illegal. It is very dangerous. Since the surfaces are so close to the ground — generally between 1,000 to 2,000 feet (305 to 610 m) high — there is no room for error in deploying the parachute. Jumpers also risk hitting the objects from which they jump.

## TAKE A NUMBER

When a BASE jumper has jumped off one of each type of object, he or she can apply for a number from the U.S. BASE Association. The number tells them how many people have completed the challenge before them.

Extreme athletes enjoy the thrill of a crazy stunt, such as BASE jumping off a cliff over a body of water, because it is so dangerous.

# CHAPTER 4

# Wingsuit Flying

For centuries humans have been trying to figure out how to fly like birds. While this is still something outside of our reach, extreme athletes have come very close with wingsuit flying. This highly specialized form of skydiving involves a unique suit. This suit allows a flyer to soar over the earth before deploying a parachute and landing.

The secret to flying is the wingsuit itself. Wingsuits work because of the physics of flying. They are designed to increase the surface area of the flyer. Webbing between the legs and under each arm create "wings." The webbing is made of strong fabric and has special **air cells** that inflate when they catch the air.

When an athlete wears a wingsuit, he or she is able to **descend** at a slower rate and stay in freefall longer. He or she can also travel much greater distances. Unlike skydivers, who fall more vertically, wingsuit flyers travel over a longer horizontal distance as they descend. The longest distance a flyer has glided is 11 miles (17.7 km)!

**air cell**—a pocket in fabric that can fill up with air, allowing something to take flight

**descend**—to move from a higher place to a lower place

During long wingsuit flights, athletes can get a beautiful view of the earth below.

# CHAPTER 5

# Extreme Ziplining

Lots of skill and practice is required for many extreme sports. But there are a few activities in which anyone in good physical shape can participate. One of these sports is extreme ziplining.

Zipline tracks stretch over valleys and canyons. Metal cables and pulleys allow a person wearing a harness to speed from the top of the track to the bottom. Zipliners can reach speeds up to 100 miles (161 km) per hour.

Like many other extreme sports, ziplining began as a practical way to travel. Even in ancient times, people used ziplines as transportation to cross difficult **terrain** or reach **remote** areas.

For extreme zipliners, two main factors are speed and distance. Zipliners get a thrill from speeding as fast as possible along the cables. They can reach higher speeds when tracks are longer. The longest zipline in the world, Puerto Rico's "The Monster," is nearly 1.5 miles (2.4 km) long.

**terrain**—the surface of the land
**remote**—far away, isolated, or distant

In New Zealand, zipliners can go on an ecotour to look at the landscape while gliding.

# AROUND THE WORLD

Some of the world's most extreme ziplines are found in Arenal Volcano National Park in Costa Rica, Sun City in South Africa, and Flight of the Gibbon in Thailand.

# CHAPTER 6

# Gliding

Many people want to know what it feels like to fly without the help of an airplane. Gliding is one way to do that. A non-powered aircraft gives them the lift to leave the ground. The best type of non-powered aircraft to use is a **sailplane**.

The most popular gliding sports are general gliding, paragliding, and hang gliding. When gliding competitively, gliders compete for distance, speed, and height gained.

## Paragliding

When paragliding, the glider is strapped into a harness. The harness is attached to a rectangular parachute with cords called lines. To begin, the glider inflates the air cells on the parachute. Then he or she runs down a slope until there is enough speed to launch into flight. He or she flies at a speed of about 12 miles (19 km) per hour.

Parachutes are made out of strong, tear-proof **synthetic** fabric with air pockets that fill with wind. The parachute does not have a **rigid** frame. It can be steered by the paraglider's body position and use of the lines.

Extreme paragliders can fly long distances. Many can glide more than 100 miles (161 km) during a single flight. In competitions, paragliders show off their skills by flying to points far away. Average paragliding speeds are 17 to 28 miles (27 to 45 km) per hour.

Paragliding can give athletes a bird's-eye view of beautiful landscapes and mountains.

**sailplane**—a light, unpowered aircraft that can be lifted up by the air

**synthetic**—something that is made by people rather than found in nature

**rigid**—inflexible; not easy to bend

sailplane

parachute

The world's best hang gliders enter competitions such as the Grininko Hang Gliding Competition in Crimea, Ukraine.

# Hang Gliding

Hang gliding is very similar to paragliding, but there are some big differences. The most important difference is the aircraft itself. Hang gliders have rigid frames made of hard metal. They are covered with lightweight fabric, such as nylon or Dacron. Because of this structure, the gliders cannot control their flight the same way that paragliders do. Someone who is hang gliding must shift his or her body weight to steer the aircraft.

Early hang gliders were made of heavy materials and were difficult to steer. A major improvement in steering came when swing seats were developed. Today, even after much improvement, gliders are still looking for ways to improve the aircraft. Thanks to new designs, modern hang gliders can have a **glide ratio** of more than 20 to 1. This means that for every 20 feet (6 m) forward a hang glider sails, the aircraft descends 1 foot (0.3 m). This is a great improvement from the first glide ratios which were about 3 to 1!

Hang gliders can travel faster than paragliders, up to about 62 miles (100 km) per hour. They can also travel long distances. The best hang gliders have traveled more than 300 miles (483 km).

**glide ratio**—the ratio of how far an object glides horizontally to how far it drops vertically

# CHAPTER 7

# Highlining

The extreme sport of highlining comes from a much tamer activity known as slacklining. In slacklining, a person attaches a thin strip of nylon webbing between two fixed points, often the bases of tree trunks. Then, starting at one end, the slackliner walks to the other end of the line.

Highlining raises the stakes. The line is dozens — or even hundreds — of feet (meters) off the ground. Any misstep could mean severe injury or death.

One thing that makes highlining so difficult is the line itself. The nylon material is not sturdy like a balance beam. Because it is flexible, it bends with the highliner's weight. The line is also very thin, usually about 1 inch (2.5 centimeters) thick. It is essential that the highliner attaches the line properly to anchors on each end so that the line does not fall. The line must be anchored to a sturdy object that can support the highliner's weight.

Balance is the other challenge highliners face. They do not use anything to help them keep their balance while crossing the line. Instead, highliners rely on stretching out their arms and having a good sense of their own body. Balancing on a highline can be difficult to master.

## EXTREME FACT!

Highliners come together every year for the Urban Highline Festival in Poland.

It is important to anchor the line securely on objects that can support the weight of a person.

Highlining allows people to see amazing parts of the world from a new perspective — and with an added adrenaline rush. People have set up highlines all over the world. Deserts, mountains, water, and canyons all offer different highline experiences. Some of the most famous places for highlining include Yosemite Falls, California; eastern France; Utah; southern California; and Kjerag Lysefjorden, Norway.

No matter how extreme a sport, competitive athletes are always looking for ways to take things to the next level. They want to cross longer lines at taller heights. Danny Menšík and Nathan Paulin hold the record for crossing the world's longest highline. This highline is located in Aiglun, France, and is a whopping 3,346.5 feet (1,020 m) long!

Professional highliner Faith Dickey has paved the way for women in this extreme sport.

Every year there are slackline festivals held around the world in many beautiful locations. In 2017 a festival was held in Barão de Cocais, Brazil.

# DEAN POTTER

One of the most important athletes in extreme sports was Dean Potter. Potter was a climber, highliner, BASE jumper, and wingsuit flyer. He was not only skilled but also creative. Sometimes, he borrowed from different extreme sports to create one thrilling adventure. For example, he combined wingsuit flying and BASE jumping. Potter was well known in the highlining world because of his daring adventures without safety nets. Potter died in a BASE jumping accident in 2015 after the parachute of his wingsuit didn't deploy.

# CHAPTER 8

# ZERO·G Experience®

In extreme air sports, the sky is the limit. But extreme adventurers have set their sights even higher — outer space! To get a feel for weightlessness without leaving Earth, they can join a ZERO-G Experience®.

The ZERO-G Experience® takes place on a specially designed airplane. Once the plane flies to a height of 24,000 feet (7,315 m), the pilot begins a series of maneuvers called **parabolas**. During each parabola, passengers in the plane experience 20 to 30 seconds of weightlessness. In total, a ZERO-G Experience® plane will fly 15 parabolas per session.

There is little gravity in space, and a ZERO-G Experience® feels a lot like space travel. While weightless, people can float, flip, and soar in ways that are not possible in any other place on Earth. This is truly the new frontier for extreme air sports.

The ZERO-G Experience® is currently used for recreation. Participants do not need to be extreme athletes. Anyone in good health can participate, and kids as young as 8 years old have done ZERO-G. After taking a brief class, they are ready to be weightless.

There is plenty of room for advancement in the future of ZERO-G and other extreme sports. Without creativity, bravery, and a little technology, air sports wouldn't be the extreme activities we know today.

**parabola**—a curve that follows the shape of an object that is thrown into the air and falls down

Before going up into the air, participants complete a course to learn all about ZERO-G.

## EXTREME FACT!

During a ZERO-G Experience®, a person undergoes a total of about eight minutes of weightlessness.

# Glossary

**air cell** (AYR sell)—a pocket in fabric that can fill up with air, allowing something to take flight

**altitude** (AL-ti-tood)—how high a place is above sea level

**descend** (dee-SEND)—to move from a higher place to a lower place

**glide ratio** (GLIDE RAY-shee-oh)—the ratio of how far an object glides horizontally to how far it drops vertically

**parabola** (par-AB-oh-la)—a curve that follows the shape of an object that is thrown into the air and falls down

**remote** (ri-MOHT)—far away, isolated, or distant

**rigid** (RIJ-id)—inflexible; not easy to bend

**sailplane** (SAYL-playn)—a light, unpowered aircraft that can be lifted up by the air

**synthetic** (sin-THET-ik)—something that is made by people rather than found in nature

**terrain** (tuh-RAYN)—the surface of the land

# Read More

**Hamilton, Sue L.** *Daredevil.* Minneapolis: A&D Xtreme, 2015.

**Luke, Andrew.** *Air Sports.* Adventurous Outdoor Sports. Broomall, Penn.: Mason Crest, 2017.

**Loh-Hagan, Virginia.** *Extreme Skydiving.* Ann Arbor, Minn.: Cherry Lake Publishing, 2016.

**Orr, Tamra B.** *Extreme Skysurfing.* Sports on the Edge! New York: Marshall Cavendish, 2014.

# Internet Sites

FactHound offers a safe, fun way to find Internet sites related to this book. All of the sites on FactHound have been researched by our staff.

Here's all you do:

Visit *www.facthound.com*

Type in this code: 9781515778615

Check out projects, games and lots more at
**www.capstonekids.com**

# Index